Debt

poems by

David Armand

Blue Horse Press
Redondo Beach, California
2018

Copyright © 2018 by David Armand
All rights reserved.
Printed in the United States of America

Cover art: "Chaser's Bar, Keansburg,"
by Jeffrey Alfier

Editors: Jeffrey and Tobi Alfier

ISBN: 978-0692144770

Other Books by David Armand

My Mother's House   Texas Review Press (2016)
The Gorge   Southeast Missouri State University Press (2015)
The Deep Woods   Blue Horse Press (2015)
Harlow   Texas Review Press (2013)
The Pugilist's Wife   Texas Review Press (2011)

Table of Contents

Acknowledgments

Grateful acknowledgment is made to the editors of the following journals in which some of these poems originally appeared, sometimes in slightly different form.

Eunoia Review: "After Quail Hunting," "Fire"
Flash Fiction Press: "Wallet"
Foxglove Journal: "Cologne"
Furtive Dalliance: "Bail," "Coach," "Garden," "Go-Kart"
Muddy River Poetry Review: "Truck"
The Penmen Review: "Anger," "Rabbit Cage"
Poetry South: "Debt"
San Pedro River Review: "The Hitchhiker"
Town Creek Poetry: "Bridge"

This book is dedicated to my family, all of them.

Wallet

Christmas morning and you've already opened up all your gifts:
the accumulation of a meager year, but still you're glad
for this airtight ammunition box made of industrial plastic,
even though you have no shotgun shells to put in it yet
and your .410's locked away in your father's closet.

You're looking at this camouflage-green box and imagining
it filled with rows of ammunition, and then chambering
one of those red plastic shells in your gun's dark barrel
in hopes of killing a duck or a squirrel or a rabbit.

This is when your father comes into your room.
He looks down at you looking down at that box
and he asks you how much money you got for Christmas
that year. You tell him (it's really not that much
since you're only nine and your family's poor anyway)
and then he asks if he can borrow it.

Although he doesn't say, you already know
what it's for, but you tell him "yes" anyway.
What else are you supposed to say?
He promises he'll pay you back. With interest.
As though that makes handing over your Christmas money
so that your dad can buy beer with it a better deal.

You open your Velcro wallet—the sound like tearing
a sheet of construction paper in a quiet classroom—
and you pull out the crumpled ones and fives.
He takes them without ever looking directly at you.
"Thanks, babe," he says. "I'll pay you back. Don't worry."

Then he leaves your room, head down, headed

to whatever dark place would be open on Christmas
and serving alcohol to men without families
and indiscriminately to those who left theirs at home
beside a wilting Christmas tree doused with lights.

Power

The boy's father never kept a bank account
so each month on payday he'd cash
his checks at the grocery store
for a fee.

      Then the boy would watch
him as he counted out stacks
of tens, twenties, and hundreds
on the wobbly kitchen table,
putting it all on top of the refrigerator
in a fat envelope,

          which got smaller
and smaller as the month wore on:
all those wrinkled bills disappearing
like air slowly leaking from an old tire
or water dripping from a rusty faucet—
things that would be better off fixed
if only there was enough to pay for it all.

But there never was.

            So that one day,
when a man in dark blue overalls
came to cut their power off,
the boy watched his mother beg:
I have kids, she'd said.
How are they gonna do their homework?
She was crying.

          The man ignored her,
but the boy could've sworn

from where he was watching
out his bedroom window
that he looked ashamed
of the job he came to do,
seemed embarrassed to be there
as he flipped the switch and sent
them all into darkness.

Rabbit Cage

My brother and I are playing outside
while our dad nails together the frame
for a rabbit cage. It's for our sister
who's out at the store with Mom.
They've taken the only car we have:
a blue Pinto we rent for sixty dollars
a week, a car so small my brother and I
have to ride in the hatchback trunk
when we take my sister to school
in the mornings. It's always cold
back there, even with the heater on.

We write our names on the glass.

Anyway, in the midst of the noise
of hammer against wood and nail,
we hear my father grunt in pain.
Then we hear him calling for help.

We run over to see he's nailed
his hand to the side of the cage.
How he did this I'll never know.
But he is losing a lot of blood,
his face is pale, his eyes are rolled
up to their white and bloodshot rims.

We help him get loose.

When our mom and sister get home,
they seem hard pressed to puzzle out
the rabbit cage leaning on its side,
but after a few minutes of explaining,

we all squeeze back into the blue Pinto
and drive to the hospital, sit there
for hours, then go back home, taking
turns in the one tiny bathroom,
washing ourselves and getting
ready for the next long day ahead,
as if all of this has happened before
and will continue to happen again
so long as we are poor and have
to do so much with so little.

Economics

Sometimes my father rolled his own cigarettes
with cheap tobacco he bought by the pound
from Walgreens.
                          It came in big yellow bags,
like dog food, but with a flimsy plastic window
in front so that you could see what was inside.

It was cheap, that tobacco, but it yielded
more cigarettes for your money,
and that's all that mattered to my father,
a man who grew up and died poor.

The last time I saw him I was nineteen
and had been an on-again-off-again smoker myself,
ever since I was twelve and stole a pack of Carltons
from my grandmother, who bought them by the carton.

I smoked my first one in the woods behind our trailer
and then kept the rest of the pack in a Cracker Jack tin
under a rotten log. I would smoke one every day
after school until the pack was gone; then I buried
the empty box in the dirt.

                          When I was eighteen,
I started smoking Camels or sometimes Marlboros
since you could get two packs for the price of one
from a place called River Forest Mart in Covington,
and because Mickey Rourke and Sean Penn smoked
those and I thought they looked cool doing it.

Eventually I gave it up, though.
                          But not before a meeting

I had for work one night, which ended
at one of my colleagues' houses,
and where she offered me a cigarette
from a stash she kept in her freezer.

I smoked it, flicking the ashes
into a black plastic ashtray, then blowing
out that last cold drag of smoke—
one I would never have to pay for again.

Cologne

It was a mirrored, wooden cabinet
hung at about eye-level so he could see
himself before he left for work
in the morning, when it was still dark out
and everyone else was asleep and warm.

But he kept nothing but cologne in there,
bottles and bottles of it: Brut, Old Spice,
Pierre Cardin, English Leather, Coty Musk,
Stetson, Aqua Velva, Afta, Skin Bracer,
Preferred Stock, Aspen. Cheap stuff

his kids gave him, or maybe he bought it
himself at the drugstore for under ten bucks
so he'd have some variety in the morning,
some choice in how he presented himself
to a world where he didn't have many choices,

a world that was hard on him, and one he'd leave
far too soon: just after a meager Christmas one year
at only forty-two years old, all those cheap bottles
collecting dust now, their contents slowly evaporating
until the day comes when nothing at all is left of him.

Shotgun

It was a Remington .410 Wingmaster
I'd owned since I was a boy.
I had learned to shoot with it.
First at beer cans and then at paper targets
nailed to a pine tree in our back yard.
Then finally using it to kill
more quail and squirrels and ducks
than you could shake a stick at,
as my father would've said.

My father. The man who walked
into a pawnshop one day
with me following closely behind him
as he went up to the counter
and hocked every gun he had,
just so that we could eat that month.

What does that sort of memory teach a boy,
if not to do the same thing himself one day?
Twenty years later when his own family's hungry—
leaving them out in the car as he goes inside
to pawn the only gun he has left,
which he had used once to bring down a squirrel
as it scampered up the side of an oak tree
before it was filled with a bunch of tiny pellets.

Bail

The first time my father was arrested
we put up our property for his bond.
After that when we couldn't keep him
out of jail—DWIs, resisting arrest,
driving under a suspended license,
illegal possession of a firearm,
intimidation, disorderly conduct, assault—
we had to let him stay there
until he saw a judge. The final verdict
was five years. My dad had done time
before, so I was surprised to find him
sitting at the kitchen table the night before
we dropped him off to start his sentence,
smoking and sobbing quietly. He flicked
his ashes into a coffee cup that was stained
brown from years of use, but also neglect.

Debt

A knock on the front door as you play in the den
with your brother and your older sister.
Your mom gets up from the sofa to answer it
and you hear her screaming as some man pushes
his way into the house, a gun pointing
at her head. She tells you and your siblings
to run, hide under the bed.

           And you can't remember
anything else from that morning except for this:
the man asking where your father was, saying
he's there to collect some money, a payment
on a payday loan. But your father's at work
and probably wouldn't pay this man anyway,
even if he was here and could see his kids
hiding in a quivering row underneath their bed.
Like the three little pigs in that story your mom reads,
the one about the big bad wolf who blows down
all their poorly-made houses—all except for one.

Go-Kart

When we were in the third grade, I remember,
my parents bought my brother and me
a Go-Kart to ride around in the fields
behind our house.

It cost three-hundred-and-fifty dollars,
but we were so poor that we had to pay
on it in installments. Twenty-five bucks a month.

I remember, too, the man who would take
our checks: he had a handlebar mustache
which he kept waxed into two curled points
like the marks on the sides of those shoes
that all the other kids at school had
but which we couldn't afford, either.

(We got our shoes from Payless.)

                          Anyway:
It was a one-seater with a Briggs & Stratton
on the back, and we took turns going
back and forth—over and over—from our yard
to our grandma's, whose trailer was two doors down.

The times when my dad would run out of cigarettes
and had no way to get to the store, he'd take the Go-
Kart to my grandma's so he could bum some from her,
even though she smoked Carltons, and he had to tear
off the perforated filter just to get enough nicotine
to equal half of what he got from one of his Marlboros.

I remember all of these things—and this too:

how the only time I ever told my dad I loved him
his face turned red and he just looked
away from me and said, "I'm not going anywhere, babe.
What the hell are you telling me that for?"

And I remember that I never said that to him again.
Not even as he was dying ten years later
and I should have told him, but couldn't bring
myself to make the words.

                    So today I remember this:
Just last week, I was racing my kids on Go-Karts
not much different from the one I used to have as a boy,
how the engines buzzed behind us as my wife watched,
took pictures with her phone. All of this
as we went around that slick oval track
over and over again, but always ending up
in the same place where we had started.

14

Bridge

We're driving across the Causeway,
twenty-four miles over black water,
and making our way to New Orleans
for a late-night Mardi Gras parade
when a car passes us on our left
and the passenger flicks a cigarette
out the window. It hits our windshield
and a slew of orange sparks spreads
over the glass like a puff of snow.

From the back seat, we hear our dad
cursing and then see the orange tip
of the push-button lighter as he lights
his own cigarette and starts puffing
on it wildly. He's speeding up the car,
trying to catch the one that just passed,
our mom pulling on his arm for him
to slow down before he gets us killed.

When he finally catches up to them,
he rolls down the window, the rush
of air coming in cold and with rain,
and then he flicks his own cigarette
out at the car that just passed us.

Revenge. The driver and passenger
look confused as the orange sparks
bloom over their hood now, and die.
Then we slow back down, headlights
from the cars behind us growing larger
and larger in our sideview mirrors
as the lake on either side spreads out
flat as a fallow field in autumn.

The Hitchhiker

My father was coming home.
It was three in the morning,
and he was driving down Hwy 47
in Chalmette, Louisiana.
This was after twelve long hours
of trawling for shrimp
in Lake Borgne and the bayous
surrounding it—returning
with his nets empty.

Then, in that early morning dark,
he saw a hunched-over old man
hitchhiking on the side of the road.
My father slowed, then stopped.
Decided to pick him up.
After all, the man looked harmless,
not to mention it was cold.

The cracked domelight glowed
as the hitchhiker got in the cab,
and my father saw his dirty clothes,
long beard—the smell of him—
and thought he was doing
a good thing: until he pulled
off and the old man grabbed
a knife from his coat.

He held its rusty blade against
my father's throat, told him
to give over his wallet.
So my father leaned forward,
not saying a word, one hand

still on the steering wheel—
and reaching with the other
as if carefully going for
what the old man wanted.

But he grabbed a gun instead,
pushing its cold barrel
against the old man's head, knocking
away the knife, slamming the brakes
and forcing the hitchhiker out
before his truck even came to a stop.

And I still imagine that old man
on the cold gravel shoulder,
watching the red taillights
from my father's truck
diminish now into a single point,
astonished at his turn of bad luck
and wondering who in the hell
had just picked him up.

Garden

It was around thirty feet long
by twelve feet wide, framed with railroad ties
that smelled like creosote as they baked
in the sun. They were stacked in threes,
the space inside filled with damp leaves,
eggshells, coffee grounds, and horse manure,
all covered with a layer of fresh topsoil.

I don't know why my dad built it, or even wanted to
in the first place. He didn't really like being outside
except to maybe sit on the porch and drink Budweisers
from a can. Smoke cigarettes.

But one year I remember him setting up a trellis
made out of chickenwire and some wooden stakes
which edged the garden and was eventually filled
with vines from tomato plants and squash.

He grew corn and cantaloupe, merlitons, red potatoes,
even planted a row of peach trees on the other side
of the yard, their branches laden with fruit
and drooping onto the grass so that we couldn't fill
our old wheelbarrow fast enough.

Most of them rotted.

He had a fig tree too
which eventually grew higher than our roof,
its gigantic leaves covering the satellite dish.
We'd have to go outside and trim them back
just so that we could get a signal inside.

He grew all of these things so fast we could never eat it
and so he brought the fruit to work in Walmart bags
and gave them to his coworkers.

My mom canned
some of the figs in little glass Mason jars and made
pepper jelly and fig preserves, which I would use
on peanut butter sandwiches when we ran
out of Smucker's.

Despite this overabundance
and the not-knowing-what-to-do
with all the things he grew,
my dad kept gardening anyway.
Kept at it for several years, furrowing
the rows of damp soil every new season.

It was like an addiction.

He worked every evening in his jeans and flip-flops,
a cool can of Bud cratered in the grass next to him.

And never too far out of reach.

Coach

The first day of class he made fun of me
for my long hair so I didn't like him much.
A few weeks in and nothing had changed
until one day he started talking about his child-
hood, how his father bought whiskey instead
of paying the bill to heat their house, how he
had only one pair of brown Dickies to wear
to school for the entire year and if they got holes
in them, then tough luck.
                                    He told us about the times
his father hit him, and how finally he had moved out
and signed up for the army. Vietnam. His buddies
over there dying in his lap like damp sacks of rice.
How he finally ended up here, teaching kids like me
with long hair and grease under their fingernails,
I guess I'll never know.

Fire

1.

I was younger than my kids are now,
probably by at least a couple of years,
when I told my brother to stick a key
in the electrical socket in our room.
I sat behind him and pretended
we were driving down some highway
when he stuck in the key, and the sparks
shot out blue and white
with yellow traces of flame crawling
up the wainscoting, turning it black,
almost as dark as the room became
when the breaker finally tripped
and set the whole house to darkness.

The stars were buckshot across the sky
outside our square little window
which let in a cylinder of moonlight
while we sat there stunned and blank-faced
as mannequins, our reddening cheeks
waxing in the now-crackling firelight.

Before we could even move, me or him,
let alone call out for help,
our dad came in and pushed us both back
and, in what seemed the same motion, grabbed
one of our plastic swords from off the floor
and knocked the key from the socket
until it lay black-edged on the carpet
like a scrap of steel discarded from its forge.

2.

Years later, when we were both teenagers,
my brother and I and two of our cousins
were pulling Black Cats from the single fuse
that held them together, then tossing
the individual fireworks into a metal lid
that we had pried from a tin of popcorn
which someone had given us that Christmas.
I'm not sure why, but one of our cousins lit
the Black Cat he was holding, then pitched
it into the lid with the unlit ones,
which all seemed to be waiting there
like a nest of angry black moccasins.

The little explosions, cumulatively, were loud,
the noise doubled by the echo from the metal lid.
And this time it was our mom, not our father,
running into the room to see what we had done.

The ceiling was already black. The gray smoke
was hanging around our shoulders and chests now
as it made its slow ascent up and then out of our room
through an open window and then into the yard.

3.

Now that I'm a father, I'm thinking about these things
after my kids brought a lit candle into their room today
and left it there—those same flames from my childhood
crawling up their wall as I ran into the house,
the smoke already thick and black,
chuffing up against the ceiling like a dark cumulus cloud,
as if it were being puffed out from a squeezed accordion,

the smoke alarm buzzing, my lungs hot and clenching.
I pushed things out of the way that were within the fire's reach—
a dresser, a nighttable, some stuffed animals, a few pillows.
I didn't know what else to do.

Then a man who had been doing some work in our yard
was in the room with me, not saying anything
as he sprayed a mist of sodium bicarbonate
from a chipped, red fire extinguisher he had in his truck,
suffocating the fire as though it had never been.
Now all that was left was the thick smoke,
and me still standing there in the dark—by myself
since that man had walked back out, still not saying anything.
I opened the window so I could let the rest of the smoke clear.

Anger

Every weekend my father sat
on the sofa all day watching
movies like *Lethal Weapon,*
Platoon, Lonesome Dove,
Tombstone, and all five *Rockys*
back to back.

          His favorite one
was *The Abyss* with Ed Harris
and Mary Elizabeth Mastrantonio
and sometimes he'd watch it—
rewind the tape he'd rented
from John's Curb Market,
which was down the road in Folsom
and where he also bought
cigarettes, beer, and once or twice
a Slush Puppy for my brother and me—
and then he'd watch it again.

You could hear the old VCR
humming and clicking
all the way from our room
at the other end of the trailer
as my father rewound the tape
and watched that movie about
underwater oil rig workers
who encounter an alien species
as they try to help disarm
a nuclear warhead on a submarine—
all while a vicious hurricane spins
above the surface of the ocean.

He'd drink can after can of Bud
and smoke Marlboro reds,
flecking the old coffee table—
which was made out of a hatch
door from a boat he'd once owned—
with gray ashes.
    Times when the batteries
in the remote controller stopped working,
he'd yell for my brother or me to come
into the den to change the channel for him
or turn up the sound, fast forward the previews
for the upcoming features he didn't care about.
"Oh, *boys*," he'd yell. "Get your asses in here."
We always thought we were in trouble at first,
but then we'd get to the den and he'd just tell
us what to do. It was embarrassing for everyone.

Other times when we had to walk past him
to get in the kitchen for something to eat,
we always ducked beneath the TV screen
so we wouldn't get in his way, but even still
he'd pop up from his spot on the sofa,
unpredictably and without warning sometimes,
and he'd yell, "What the *hell* are you looking
at, son? You want to *fight*? *Huh*? You think
you can whip my ass?"
      "No," we'd say back,
softly, like stepping over a rat trap, or holding
a loaded shotgun, keeping it pointed at the sky
so if it accidentally went off, it wouldn't kill anyone.
We never bothered mentioning that we hadn't looked
at him at all, had purposely kept our eyes on our feet.

We'd just keep moving, hoping he wouldn't follow,

25

that he'd just sit back down and leave us alone
and watch his damn movies like we didn't even exist.

Play

My father didn't play with us much when we were kids.
Our mom said he wasn't really the playful *type*, never was,
so we just had to take what we could get from him.

Which sometimes meant letting him lob softballs
at us from atop the trampoline, or holding us
under water in the pool for just a little bit too long.
I remember the panic just before breaking the skin
of the water's cool, chlorinated surface, then hearing
him laugh in that way which could only be funny
if you were on the right side of the joke: we never were.
He always let us go—eventually—but the promise
of danger and risk when it came to playing
with our father tugged at everything we did,
like an undertow, a threat more felt than seen.

This also meant letting our father win at things
so he wouldn't get mad, like that one time
we beat him at basketball and he punished us
on our knees, the granules of driveway concrete
pressing into our skin as we tried to figure out
what we had done wrong. Eventually we learned.
After that we always made sure to lose, fumbling
the ball around until he had a solid lead. He told
us we'd get better if we practiced, if we'd just stop
wasting so much time in our room. Playing Nintendo.
Or whatever it was he thought we did in there all day.

After Quail Hunting

In this picture, a .410's in my hand,
pointing skyward. I'm wearing
camouflage. I'm eight years old.
In my left hand, I'm holding
a couple of quail that we shot
in a field behind our single-wide—
the same trailer where I once locked
myself in one of the bedroom closets
and was too afraid to call out for help
so I just struggled with the door
until my uncle finally heard the noise.
He came in from where he was sitting
in the den watching the Saints game on TV
and pulled the door open to let me out.

I remember how incredibly sad he looked
that I hadn't asked for help or anything,
how instead I'd just kept pushing
on that cheap, brown wooden door
over and over and over as if it might
open on its own and let me go free.

And I can still remember those quail.
How we flushed them from the weeds
and how they rose up into the sky
like steam coming off a stack of dishes
sitting in the drainboard, freshly-washed
and waiting overnight in the dark
for someone to come along and put
them away where they belonged.

The Cast

When I was twelve I broke my wrist
and had to get a cast put over it until it healed.
That thing went all the way up to my shoulder,
making my whole arm the shape of a crooked L.

I couldn't eat, couldn't write, couldn't even bathe
without a significant amount of effort, so how on earth
was I supposed to shoot my .410, I wondered,
if I wanted to go duck hunting with my father?

My dad's solution was simple: he just cut the cast
halfway off, using a rusty hacksaw blade to slice
through the plaster, its dust like snow
piling up on the floor of the tool shed,
the cotton that was wrapped around my skin
torn apart like strands of matted horse hair.

*

When we went back to the doctor
so that I could have the cast properly removed,
the man was astounded—no, disgusted—
by what my father had done to me.
He told him as much. He said my arm
would never have a chance to heal correctly
thanks to my dad and his poor parenting.
What an injustice, the doctor said,
shaking his head and sucking at his teeth.

Then I listened to his tiny electric saw
as it went through the rest of the cast and pulled it

from my weak and skinny arm, its high-pitched buzz
whining as the rest of the plaster finally came free.

I could tell my father was embarrassed as we left,
but that doctor was wrong: my arm healed up just fine
and it had helped me kill a nice little passel of ducks that year,
despite the injustice he thought my dad had caused me.

Truck

It was a tan Mazda B2200 that my dad bought
stripped down for under eight grand. He wrecked
it not long after he got it, but still drove
it anyway, getting pulled over more than once
and taken in for DWIs or otherwise
driving without a license.

And this is what he kept inside of it:
a sawed-off shotgun under the bench seat,
a pack of Marlboro reds, a Bowie knife
in the glove compartment, cans of Budweiser,
a box of Luden's wild cherry cough drops,
handkerchiefs, folded-up maps, Bic lighters,
pencils, tools, his suspended driver's license.

When he gave the truck to me years later,
the seats were torn and I had to cover them
with a quilt I found in one of our closets.
I put in a cheap radio and some speakers
behind the seat, the wires draped over the dash
like cobwebs.
            The truck had over 300,000 miles
on it and by the time I got rid of it, I'd turned
over the odometer so that it showed all zeros.

Mischief

An image: two metal garbage cans on either side of the street.
They're tied together by their squeaky handles with jute twine
found in someone's father's garage next to a can
of half-empty Miller Lite.

          The string is old, which is good
because it droops loose enough so the tired drivers
heading home won't see it, won't know what the hell
just happened when the cans slam against their cars
as that string pulls taut and metal collides with metal,
a loud scraping noise.
          Something unnatural but thrilling
to the group of fifteen-year-old boys
hiding behind the bushes off to the side, the orange glow
of their stolen cigarettes lighting up their faces
and eyes as the brake lights come on
and the driver gets out from behind the wheel,
cursing as those kids just try to hold in their laughter.
Not an easy thing to do having fun like this.
And when the car pulls off they'll do it all over again.

You should know that one of these boys is my father.
He's the youngest of the group. Only nine and already smoking,
hanging out with these hoodlums, as his mother calls them.

And this too: that tomorrow they'll throw water balloons
into people's houses, watching the living room carpet soak
up the spill, and then running down the sidewalk
before Mrs. Ordes can see their faces well enough to tell

their fathers. Those men who come home from work tired
and pissed off, just looking for a good reason to whale

on their sons, slipping a cracked leather belt
from their greasy work pants and watching the welt
it makes on the backs of their boys' legs, something
feminine about the pink blooms of flesh.
How they blister and burn.

That's probably what they're worrying over as one of them finally
tosses in the balloon, not filled with water like they thought
(the kid who did it *said* they'd be surprised)
but a pint of white paint which spreads out over the carpet
like blood, thick and slow to move. The horror stamped
on all their faces, a silent tableau. And then the realization:
This woman standing before them knows all of their fathers,
will surely tell who did it. And they'll all have hell to pay,
a hell these boys will pass on to their own sons one day—
like Adam's curse, their pain exchanged and passed along
for when their sons do something dumb, which they'll inevitably do,
until someone stops them, says, "Come here, son. I love you."

About the Author

David Armand was born and raised in Louisiana. He has worked as a drywall hanger, a draftsman, and as a press operator in a flag-printing factory. He is currently Writer-in-Residence at Southeastern Louisiana University, where he also serves as associate editor for Louisiana Literature Press. In 2010, he won the George Garrett Fiction Prize for his first novel, *The Pugilist's Wife*, which was published by Texas Review Press. His second novel, *Harlow*, was published by Texas Review Press in 2013. In 2015, David's third novel, *The Gorge*, was published by Southeast Missouri State University Press, and his first poetry chapbook, *The Deep Woods*, was published by Blue Horse Press. David's memoir, *My Mother's House*, was published in March 2016 by Texas Review Press. David lives with his wife and two children and is working on his seventh book, *The Lord's Acre*, as well as a second memoir.

www.ingramcontent.com/pod-product-compliance
Lightning Source LLC
Chambersburg PA
CBHW051741040426
42447CB00008B/1243